KU-189-246

Play games!

Schools Library and Infomation Services

S00000693863

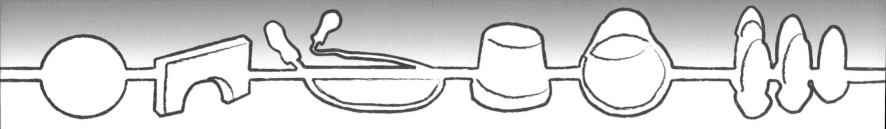

Published by Evans Brothers Limited
2a Portman Mansions
Chiltern Street
London W1U 6NR

VISIT OUR WEBSITE
www.evansbooks.co.uk

First published in paperback in 2005

All rights reserved. No part of this publication may be reproduced, stored in a retrieval system, or transmitted, in any form, or by any means, electronic, mechanical, photocopying, or otherwise, without prior permission of Evans Brothers Limited.

Consultant: Dr Naima Browne
Publisher: Su Swallow
Design: Neil Sayer
Editorial: Debbie Fox
Picture research: Julia Bird
Production: Jenny Mulvanny

British Library Cataloguing in Publication Data
Lawson, Julia
  Play games!
  1.Play - Pictorial works - Juvenile literature
  I.Title
  790
  ISBN 0237529203

© Evans Brothers Limited 2002
First published in 2002

Acknowledgements

The author and publisher would like to thank the following for their kind help:

Richard Johnson and all the staff at Southfield Primary School, London W4, the parents of the children photographed, and the children (in page order from the title page): Beatrice Tompkins, Lindsy Norville, Sammy Pratt, William Douthwaite-Hodges, Whitney Burdett, Matthew Tillyer and Alexander Evans.
The Early Learning Centre for the use of a range of their toys.

How to use this book

- Always remember that reading together should be fun!
- Reading with young children involves more than simply reading the words on the page. Talking about the pictures and ideas and linking them with children's experiences provide invaluable learning opportunities.
- Most children will enjoy an adult reading the book to them for the first time. Some children will want an adult to continue doing this, whilst others may prefer to have a go at reading the book themselves.
- Don't worry if children don't read the words that are written on the page. Young children often make up their own text! As the book becomes more familiar, children may remember the text and 'read' it back. This is an important stage in learning to read, so encourage children by being an appreciative audience!
- The book introduces new ideas and vocabulary. Don't expect children to take in everything at once. You will need to linger over the pages children find particularly interesting.
- Children learn by asking questions, so try not to rush through the book and be prepared to answer children's questions.

Activity boxes
- This book includes some ideas for activities that will deepen children's understanding of the concepts introduced. The activities range from simple rhymes to practical investigations.

Notes and suggested activities
- On pages 20/21 there is a useful reference list of storybooks, websites and videos as well as action songs and games and further activity suggestions.

The items featured on pages 10 and 11 are available from Galt Education and Pre-school, Johnsonbrook Road, Hyde, Cheshire, SK14 4QT, Tel. 08702 42 44 77, Fax 0800 056 0314, Email:enquires@galt-educational.co.uk

Play games!

Julia Lawson

Photographs by
Peter Millard

Evans Brothers Limited

DUDLEY PUBLIC LIBRARIES

L

693863   BCH

J 790

Ring a ring of roses, touch your toes and noses!

Build up tall, kick a ball.

Come and play games with us all!

This game starts off quietly...

and then gets very loud!

Sleeping Lions!
Here is a quiet game for you to play. Lie down on the floor and pretend to be asleep. Lie very still and don't move! One of you walks around to check that no one is moving. If anyone moves, they're out!

In this obstacle course we have to...

clamber over, squeeze under,

**wriggle through,
and balance carefully!**

I wonder if this tower will topple over.

Why won't it balance?

Five Red Apples
Five red apples hanging on a tree,
The juiciest apples you ever did see.
Along came the wind and gave an angry frown,
And one little apple came tumbling down.

How many apples were left on the tree?
Carry on this rhyme with four apples, three, two and one.

Balancing balls...

bowling balls...

bouncing balls...

batting balls.

Counting beads ...
one, two, three.

Marble Run!

You need some marbles, cardboard tubes and boxes. Stick the tubes to the boxes – some high and some low. Try cutting some tubes in half lengthways so that you can see your marbles as they run!

Flicking tiddlywinks into the centre can be tricky!

I need to write numbers for hopscotch.

Jumping forward, jumping back. How many times can you jump?

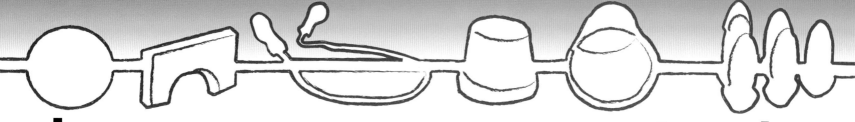

In some games we pretend to be different types of people.

Who do you like to pretend to be?

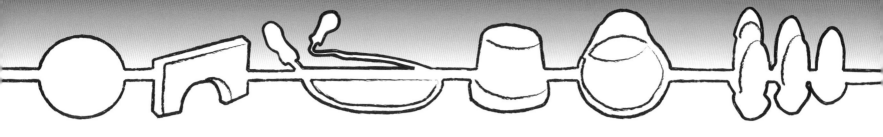

Notes and suggested activities for parents and teachers

We hope that you have enjoyed sharing this book and have tried out some of the ideas in the activity boxes. Feel free to adapt them as you wish; for example, the Sleeping Lions game on page 7 can also be played as 'Football Statues', 'Scary Monsters' and 'Favourite Animals'. Listed here are some children's storybooks, poems, games, videos, CD-Roms and websites that relate to the theme of playing games. Have fun!

Storybooks
Play with Spot, Eric Hill, Frederick Warne
Who Will Play With Me?, Michele Coxon, Happy Cat Books
Ten Play Hide-and-Seek, Penny Dale, Walker Books
Pretend You're a Cat, Jean Marzollo, Puffin
Roxaboxen, Alice McLerran, Puffin
Captain Pajamas, Bruce Whatley, Harper Collins
Cows Can't Fly, David Milgrim, Puffin
Dog's Day, Jane Cabrera, Orchard Books
Africa Calling, Nighttime Falling, Daniel Alderman, Whispering Coyote Press

On the Way Home, Jill Murphy, Macmillan
Whatever Next! Jill Murphy, Campbell Books

Song
Here is a number song that children will enjoy singing along to.

Sing a Song of Numbers (to the tune of 'Sing a Song of Sixpence')

Sing a song of numbers,
Sing them one by one,
Sing a song of numbers,
We've only just begun.
1, 2, 3, 4, 5, 6,
7, 8, 9, 10.
When we finish singing them,
We'll sing them once again!

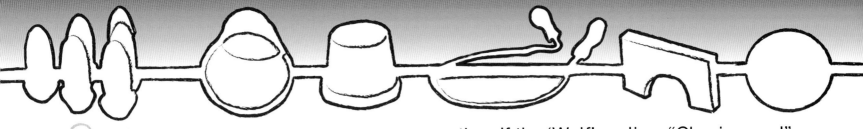

Poem

Out-time, In-time
Out-time, out-time,
Run around and shout time,
Shake it all about time,
Out-time, out-time.
In-time, in-time,
It's time to begin time,
Stop the noisy din time,
In-time, in-time.
Copyright Brian Moses 1996 in *An Orange Poetry Paintbox*, Ed John Foster, OUP 1996

Games around the world

Playing games is something children enjoy throughout the world and variations of many popular games can be found in all cultures. Here is a lovely game from Egypt.

Wolf! Wolf!
The children form a large circle around the 'Wolf' and chant, "Wolf! Wolf! What are you doing?" The 'Wolf' responds with an action sentence such as "Brushing my teeth!", "Washing my hands!" or "Combing my hair!" and the children have to imitate the action. If the 'Wolf' replies "Chasing you!" the children must run away so that the 'Wolf' can't catch them. The first person to be caught becomes the new wolf.

Videos

Ready to Play with the Tweenies, BBC Worldwide Publishing
Teletubbies *Go!*, BBC Worldwide Publishing
Jane Hissey's Old Bear and Friends *Ruff and Other Stories*, Carlton Entertainment

CD-Roms

Wake Up World! A Day in the Life of Children Around the World, Anglia Multimedia and Oxfam
The Snowman, from the book and video by Raymond Briggs, Fast Trak
Play with the Teletubbies, BBC Multimedia

Websites

www.bbc.co.uk/education/teletubbies/playground
www.bbc.co.uk/education /tweenies
www.randomhouse.com/seussville/games

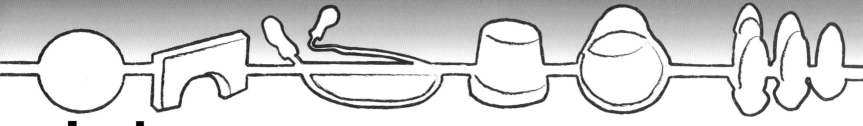

Index